CRAFT MAGIC

NORTH LIGHT BOOKS
CINCINNATI, OH

Visit our Web site at www.artistsnetwork.com for information on more resources for artists.

04   03   02   01   00   5   4   3   2   1

The catalog record for this book is available from the U.S. Library of Congress.

ISBN 1-58180-232-3

American Editor: Diane Ridley Schmitz
Editorial Production Manager: Kathi Howard
Production Supervisor: Kristen Heller
American Designer: Kevin Martin
Studio Manager: Ruth Preston

Contents

COLLAGE ✓

Paper panda

Have a rip-roaring time making this cute mother and cub collage. It's total panda-monium!

What you need:
★ Old newspapers ★ Sheet of white card (11½" x 11½")
★ Glue stick ★ Sheets of paper in white, black and gray ★ Scissors

ha ha!
What do you call a confused panda?
Bamboo-zled!

1 Tear a square of newspaper, about 10″ x 10″. Stick it down in the center of the card. Tear thin, dark strips for canes. Stick these in lines at the sides.

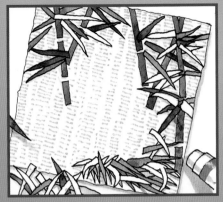

2 Rip leaf-shapes from white paper and different shades of newspaper. Stick them on the canes and at the bottom of the picture for the panda's nest.

3 Tear four black, sausage-like limbs and white ovals for a head, tummy and snout. Glue the snout on to a slightly larger gray oval. Stick the pieces down.

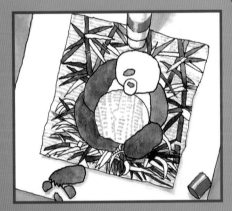

4 Glue pale newspaper strips on the tummy. Tear black paper ears, eyes, mouth, nose and arm. Snip claws at the end of the arm. Stick these down.

5 Rip a white paper bean-shape with a snout for the cub's body. Tear an arm, a leg, two ears and an eye from black paper and glue these in place.

6 Cut out some grey paper claws. Stick them on the mother's left leg. Glue a foot and four round pads in shades of gray on top. Add more leaves.

Quickdraw
...a panda

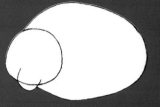

Sketch a large, oval body and a circle for the head. Add a curved line for the snout.

Draw the legs. Extend the line of the legs on the right to make stripes on the back.

Draw claws, eyes, ears, a nose and a mouth. Give lines a furry look. Shade the face and belly.

Shade the black areas with a soft pencil, leaving the feet lighter than the rest.

Monochrome magic

Try out these crafty collages with bold blacks, whites and grays.

Dig that ace!

Tear a newsprint rectangle. Stick a slightly smaller white rectangle on top. Tear one large and two small black spades. Stick them down. Glue a small newsprint spade on top of the large, black spade.

Fantasy football

Tear hexagons in black, white and grey paper, then arrange them on a circle of newsprint for a kickin' soccerball!

Penguin pair

You'll need a few scraps of orange as well as black and white paper for this penguin parent. Use newspaper for its fluffy, grey-feathered chick.

Now I'm on a roll...

It's a killer

Tear a fish-shape from black paper and add white patches for a whale of a time! In fact, killer whales are large dolphins, not whales at all!

To die for

Tear four diamonds from white paper and two from gray to make this pair of dice. Tear little circles from black paper to make the number dots.

FUN FACTS

 The giant panda lives in the bamboo forests of western China. When fully-grown, it can be as tall as a man!

Pandas eat about a third of their own body weight in bamboo shoots, stems and leaves every day! They have to eat this much as they find it hard to turn the food into energy.

Newborn pandas weigh just 5 ounces, and would fit in your hand. At birth, cubs are pink and hairless.

Shower power!

Use dried beans and a tube to make a rain-maker shaker!

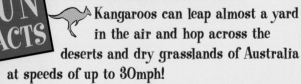

What you need:

★ Cardboard paper towel tube ★ Sheet each of orange paper ★ Pencil ★ Ruler ★ Scissors ★ Sticky tape ★ Dried beans ★ Tracing paper (optional) ★ Black felt-tip pen ★ White glue

I think I can sssee my sssplendid sssilhouette!

1 On the orange paper, draw around the end of the tube twice. Add a larger circle ½" outside each of these circles and cut them out.

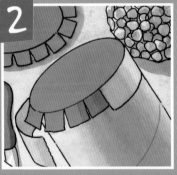

2 Make cuts around each outer circle. Cover one end of the tube with a circle. Tape the flaps down. Quarter-fill the tube with dried beans, then cover the other end.

3 Cut a piece of orange paper to fit around your tube with an overlap. Trace or copy animals from the border on to it. Color them in with a black felt-tip pen.

4 Tape one edge of the decorated paper to the tube. Wrap it around the tube and glue the other edge down. Leave it to dry, then get shaking!

FUN FACTS

Kangaroos can leap almost a yard in the air and hop across the deserts and dry grasslands of Australia at speeds of up to 30mph!

As well as kangaroos, Australian drivers have to watch out for wombats, snakes and eagles on their roads!

HOMEMADE CLAY

I always fancied being a model!

Sculpting can be cheap and easy – just make your own clay, then get down to some modeling madness!

Home-made clay fun begins before you even start your modeling! Check out the four simple recipes below – you'll find most of the ingredients in your kitchen – then get mixing!

Salt dough clay

Mix two cups of flour with three quarters of a cup of salt in a bowl. Ask an adult to gradually stir in three quarters of a cup of hot water. Then, on a lightly-floured surface, knead the dough for about six minutes.

White bread clay

Break one and a half slices of white bread (not the crusts) into small pieces. Add a tablespoon of White glue and mix with a fork until sticky. Knead the clay until it is shiny and elastic.

Sawdust clay

Mix two cups of sawdust and one cup of flour in a large bowl. Add water a little at a time, until the clay is stiff, but squishy. Then, knead the clay until everything is thoroughly mixed together.

Cinnamon clay

Mix a cup of applesauce, one and a half cups of cinnamon and a third of a cup of white glue in a bowl until it forms a ball. Put it in the fridge for half an hour. Then, roll it out on a surface sprinkled with cinnamon. Remember, your clay may smell yummy, but you mustn't eat it!

OOPS! Always ask an adult before you start. Then, cover your work surface, or work on a tray, so that the gluey clays don't ruin your table!

Keep it fresh!

Keep your clay fresh as you work. Wrap the gluey mixtures in plastic wrap, or keep the flour doughs under a damp cloth. If your mixtures get too dry, add a few drops of water. And, if they are too wet, add a little of the dry ingredient!

Something special!

When you're making your clay, you might want to brighten it up a bit. Here are three ideas for extra special ingredients.

Mix in a few spoonfuls of glitter to make super, sparkly clay.

The cinnamon clay smells great already, but to give the other clays zest, ask an adult to add a few drops of lemon or mint essence.

If you want color in your clay, add a few drops of food coloring to your mixtures.

Ordinary objects are great for shaping homemade clay.

Shape perfect stars every time with a pastry cutter.

It's easy to mold a straight line against the edge of a ruler.

Use a rolling pin to flatten out your clays.

Use a pencil to make different patterns. Or, as a perfect, miniature rolling pin!

To make a hanging hole, push a drinking straw through your clay.

Use a garlic press to make oodles of noodley hair!

A fork makes waves and adds lots of dots!

Drying time

Look below to see how long your models need to be left to dry.

The salt dough will take several days to dry. You can speed the process up by placing it in a warm airy cupboard.

Models made from white bread clay will need to be left to dry for two, or even three days before painting.

On a sunny day, you can speed up your sawdust clay drying time by placing it in the sun to bake rock-hard.

Cinnamon clay needs to dry on a cooling rack. Leave it for about two days until it changes to a light brown.

Perfect painting

When your clay creations are dry, cheer them up with a tip-top paint job.

Give your model a white acrylic paint base coat and leave it to dry. Add details, painting in funny features with a medium paintbrush and acrylic paints. When it's dry, make a gloss of one part water to one part white glue. Use a large paintbrush to paint it on. When it's dry, your model will be super-shiny!

sSSuper Cedric sSSculpture

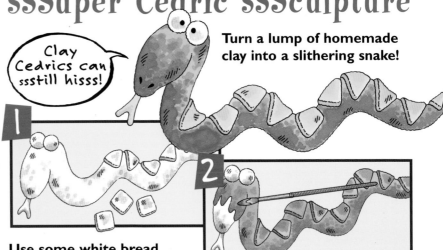

Clay Cedrics can ssstill hisss!

Turn a lump of homemade clay into a slithering snake!

1 Use some white bread clay to make a Cedric snake shape. Mold separate eyes, a tongue and diamonds for scales, then push them all firmly on to Cedric's body.

2 When it's dry, use acrylic paints and follow the painting tips to make your ssSlithery ssSculpture truly Cedric-like!

Moon monsters

Grab some odds and ends from around the house and create a crazy, clay alien invasion!

1

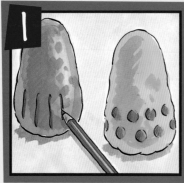

Model long, egg-shaped bodies in different-colored clay. Use both ends of a pencil to mark on stripes and spots on the bottom halves.

2

Push small cake decorations, buttons, beads and paper clips into the clay to make the aliens' faces. Use small bolts for the alien ears.

3

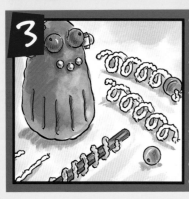

Twist pipe cleaners around a pencil to make spirals for the antennae. For the curly arms, thread beads on to the ends of the pipe cleaner spirals.

4

Cut a straw into sections and snip into them at one end to make alien arms or legs. Now have fun making an army of crazy, space creatures!

PIPE CLEANERS

When you discover how much fun bright and bendy pipe cleaners can be, you'll never believe that people use them to clean their yucky pipes!

You can buy pipe cleaners from art shops and big department stores. The bendy wire in the middle of this furry art material makes it great for creating 3-D pictures and models. Best of all, the shapes you make stay that way!

Simple shaping

Grab a pipe cleaner and practice your bending, curling and braiding skills.

A zigzag is easy. Bend your pipe cleaner one way, then bend it back. Keep bending, making each bend an equal distance apart.

To make a super, springy curl, wind a pipe cleaner around a pencil. If you want a bigger curl, wind it around a thick pen, or even your finger!

You'll need three pipe cleaners for a braid. Braid them tightly, or loosely for different effects!

It's time I got into shape!

Pipe up!

Now you know how to bend and shape, nothing can hold you back!

Use three grey pipe cleaners to bend a face and two ears. Then, cut a black pipe cleaner and attach the halves with a pink pipe cleaner to make a nose and whiskers.

Join the ends of a zigzag to make a star.

Pinch a pipe cleaner in the middle. Bend the ends around and twist them together for a heart.

Shape a flame in gold and a candle in purple. Twist the candle ends into a wick. Bend it around the flame to hold it in place.

TRICK FIX

Fix your pipe cleaner pics in place with this simple trick.

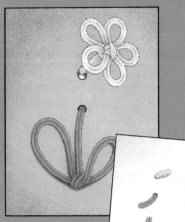

When you twist your pipe cleaner shapes, leave an end free. Make a hole in your card where you want to place your shape. Thread the end through, then bend it flat.

Your finished image will stay in place on the card!

Web-tastic winding!

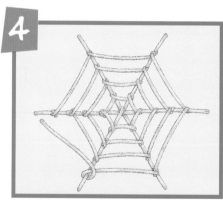

Bend and shape a spooky spider sitting on its web.

1

To make a spider, twist four black pipe cleaners together in the middle. Wind the twist into a squashed knot for the body.

2

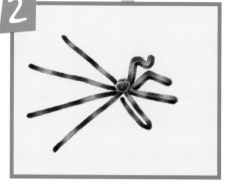

Turn the spider over and fold each of the eight legs in half. Make a bend for a knee and another for a foot in each one.

3

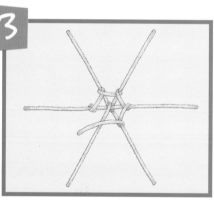

Twist three pipe cleaners in the middle. From near the center, link a pipe cleaner around each arm to make a curved ring.

4

Loop three more rings and bend the arms over the edges of a piece of card. Tuck two of the spider's feet under the rings.

Fuzzy frames

Use pipe cleaners to make frames for your ace artwork.

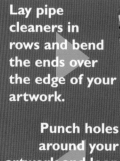

Lay pipe cleaners in rows and bend the ends over the edge of your artwork.

Punch holes around your artwork and loop the pipe cleaners through.

Lay the pipe cleaners on the card and weave them in and out of each other for a plaid effect.

PAPER WEAVING

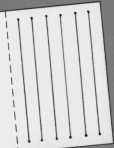

I like weaving myself around thingsss!

Weaving paper is simple and the results are amazing! Just gather together all your odd pieces of paper and cut them into strips.

Take a close look at a piece of fabric, and you will see the threads weaving over and under each other, in a crisscross pattern. You can weave paper in the same way, but you don't need a loom!

Crisscross

Divide sheets of green and yellow paper into equal strips. Cut them up. Lay three yellow strips vertically. Weave a green strip under the first yellow strip, then over and under again. Below this, weave another green strip over the first yellow strip and under, then over again. Keep weaving green and yellow strips under and over to make a complete square.

Pocket-sized

You can make your woven squares as tiny as you like just by cutting thinner strips. You could even weave a tiny mat for a dolls' house!

King-sized

Try paper weaving on a grand scale using rolled-up sheets of newspaper. Flatten them, then, using the technique on the left, weave a large mat perfect for putting your dirty boots on!

Woven greeting

Weave your best wishes into a card and pop it in the mail to a friend!

Fold a piece of card in half lengthways. Open it out. Ask an adult to cut slots in the front which start and finish ¾" from the edge.

Weave patterned paper strips in and out. Cut off any excess.

Fold the card, then write your message inside!

13

Beautiful basket

Fold a piece each of red and pink paper (3½" × 10½") in half, and use them to weave a wonderful heart basket.

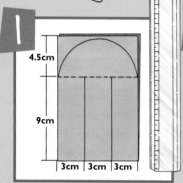

On both pieces, draw a dotted line 1¾" from the top. Draw an arc in the top area and divide the bottom into strips. Cut out the arc. Snip up the strips to make loops.

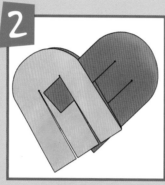

Lay the pink and red cut-out shapes side by side. Then, slide the first loop of the red paper shape between the two layers of the first loop of the pink paper shape.

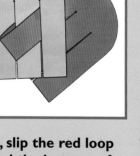

Next, slip the red loop around the bottom of the second pink loop and slide it up. Then, slip the red loop between the two layers of the third pink loop.

Slip the second red loop round the first pink loop, between the second and around the third. Follow steps 2 and 3 for the third red loop. Open it out. Glue on a handle.

Boxing clever

Turn an old cereal box into a sturdy storage box!

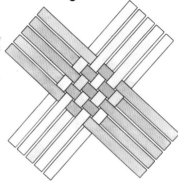

1 Open out a cereal box. Cut 10 strips 12in x 1in and six strips 15.5in x 1in. Lay five short strips design-side down. Weave five short strips through them to make a square in the middle.

2 Bend the strips on one side of the square up. Weave five of the longer strips through them to make a side. Leave the loose ends poking out on the left as far as those of the woven square.

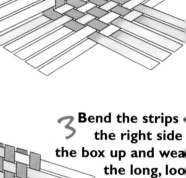

3 Bend the strips on the right side of the box up and weave the long, loose ends through them. Bend up the remaining sides and weave the ends through.

4 When all the sides of the box are woven, glue the remaining, longer strip around the top to hold all of the ends in place!

DÉCOUPAGE

Découpage (say day-koo-pauge) is the art of cutting out to decorate. Brighten up old boxes and pots by cutting out your favorite pictures and pasting them on!

You can cut out bright pictures and designs from magazines and wrapping paper. Use newspapers for neat black and white patterns and collect stamps from old letters, too. You can even buy ready-printed sheets for découpage.

Stamps

Wrapping paper

Magazine

Scissors

Newspaper

White glue

Jar of clear varnish

Outer space paste!

Use scissors to cut out lots of pictures from wrapping paper. Cut out about twice as many as you think you'll need, as they should overlap when you stick them down.

Stick your cut-out pictures down one at a time on to a sheet of card. Use a paintbrush to spread the glue evenly. Make sure that they all overlap so that there are no gaps!

OOPS!

Ask before you cut up any old magazines or newspapers!

When the glue is dry, paint on several coats of varnish with a clean paintbrush. Let the varnish dry between coats.

15

Character cutouts! Turn an old tray into a cartoon carrier!

1. Glue torn strips of colored paper to the tray. Copy or trace pictures of Marilyn and Cedric on to white paper and color them in with crayons. Cut them out.

2. Glue down each of the cut-out pictures on your tray. This is your chance to make your cut-out Marilyns and Cedrics do really crazy things! Experiment and have some fun!

3. When the glue is dry, use a clean brush to give your tray three coats of varnish. Let it dry between each coat. Now bedtime snacks will never be the same again!

Funky pots and boxes

Now that you know how to découpage, you can cover almost anything.

Stamps are always bright and colorful. Why not use them to cover a odds and ends box like this one?

Pot a plant in a funky flowerpot. Just use pieces torn from the pages of old newspapers and magazines.

Balloon bowl

All you need is paper, paste and puff to create a crazy cartoon bowl!

What you need:
- ★ Balloon ★ Old newspapers ★ Bowl
- ★ White glue ★ Water
- ★ Large paintbrush
- ★ Pin ★ Scissors
- ★ Old comics

OOPS!

Make sure each layer of wet newspaper strips is thoroughly dry before applying the next.

1 Blow up a round balloon and ask an adult to knot it. Tear an old newspaper into lots of small strips. Water down some glue (one part water, two parts glue).

2 Use the watered down glue to paste the newspaper strips over the rounded half of the balloon. When dry, paste another layer of strips on top.

3 Repeat four more times, allowing each layer to dry. Pop the balloon with a pin and peel it away from the papier-mâché. Use scissors to trim a neat rim.

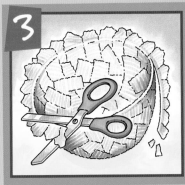

4 Tear up colorful, old comics. Paste the pieces over the bowl using watered down glue. When dry, brush glue all over to give a shiny finish.

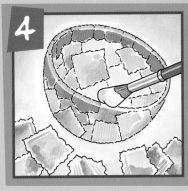

Skeleton

ABCDEFG
MNOPQR
WXYZ

Cedric's old bones

Cedric's x-ray has shown up a lot more than bones. Can you work out how many: a cups b socks c keys d cakes and e cans he's swallowed? How many bones has he got: a 160 b 149 c 75? Answers on page 22.

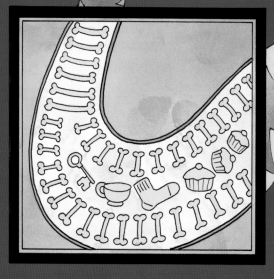

Shivering skeletons - check out this bony alphabet! Simply copy or trace the letters to make your own bone-rattling words and phrases. You've got a lot of bones to pick - so start lettering!

HIJKL STUV

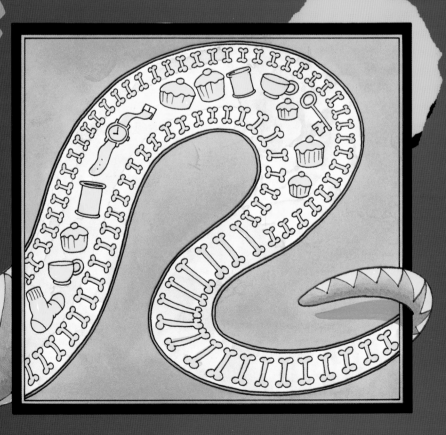

Try this

Your bony letters are perfect for treasure maps and scary keep out signs.

X To make a treasure map, first tear the edges of a sheet of paper, so it looks old.

X Draw an island and decorate your map. Use colored pencils to color it in. Press a damp teabag over the paper, to make it look even older. Leave to dry.

X Roll up your map and tie with bright ribbon.

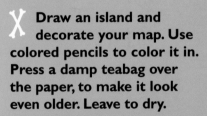

X Keep kid brothers and sisters out of your room with this bony sign. Make it from craft foam - use the picture on the left as a guide when you cut out the top and bottom.

Color class

Collage-o-saurus

That's torn it! To make this stylish stegosaurus, you'll need to tear up lots of colored paper!

What you need:
★ Sheets of colored letter size paper in pale yellow, green, pale green, orange, blue, yellow, dark blue red and white
★ Glue stick
★ Felt-tip pens in blue and black

1 Tear a pale yellow paper background. Glue on a torn-paper green strip for the grass and scraps of pale green and orange for plants and rocks.

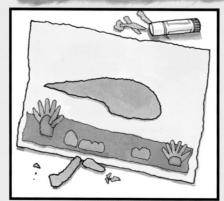

2 From blue paper, tear a large teardrop shape for the body and stick it down. Add a long strip for the neck and a short strip for the head.

3 Tear four legs from yellow paper. Make the two in the foreground slightly longer. Tear more yellow for the belly, neck and chin. Stick in place.

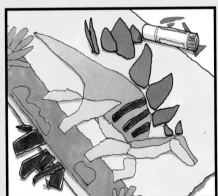

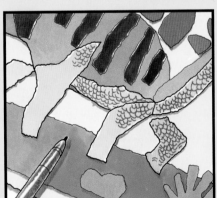

4 Now tear some dark blue paper to make bold stripes. Use red paper to make triangular spines on the back and long, bony tail spikes.

5 Use a blue felt-tip pen to draw reptilian scales all over the dinosaur's yellow legs and neck. Add baggy knees with a few curved pen strokes.

6 Use a small, torn white circle of paper to make the eye. Use a black felt-tip pen to draw an eye, nose, ear-hole, eyebrow, mouth and toes.

Tear-rific!

In prehistoric times, reptiles ruled the land – and the skies and seas, too! No one can be sure what colors these ancient creatures were, so be adventurous with these other torn-paper collage ideas.

FUN FACTS

 Dinosaurs ruled the Earth for 165 million years. Humans have been around for just two million years!

 The earliest dinosaurs were no bigger than a large dog!

Many scientists believe that the dinosaurs died out after a giant meteor hit the Earth, causing a cloud of dust that blocked out the sun.

Dinosaurs laid eggs! The first dino eggs were found in Mongolia in the 1920s. In 1978, in Montana, scientists found a nesting site with fossilized eggs and baby Maiasauras (say may-ah-saw-ras)!

King of the skies

The ancient flying reptiles are known as pterosaurs (say te-ro-saws). This dimorphodon (say dim-or-fo-don) probably used its long tail for steering in flight.

Sea-o-saurus

Ichthyosaurus (say ik-thee-o-saw-rus) means 'fish lizard'. This reptile was probably a fast swimmer. It wasn't a dinosaur though, as it didn't live on land.

Gentle giant

Triceratops (say try-se-ra-tops) was a peaceful plant-eater. Its fierce-looking horns were used for defense, not attack.

Answer to Cedric's Old Bones from page 18: **a 160**

ORIGAMI

Origami is the art of paper folding to create decorative objects. Grab a sheet of paper and have some folding fun!

Most origami shapes are of natural, living things, like birds, animals and flowers. They look hard to make, but if you follow the steps you can't go wrong. The more steps there are, the more folds you make – and the more fantastic your finished piece will be!

When you see a dotted line, fold along it.

An arrow shows you the direction to fold the paper in.

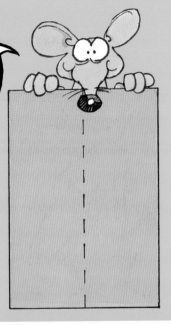

Think about what you're going to make when you choose your paper. Colored and patterned paper is great, or for a really stunning effect, choose a sheet with different colored sides. The thinner your paper is, the easier it is to fold.

Quick cup
Try your hand at this quick, origami cup. It's easy-peasy!

Take a square of paper that is a different color on both sides and fold it in half diagonally to make a triangle.

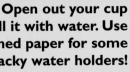

Fold the right-hand point of the triangle over, so that the tip touches the left-hand side. Then, repeat with the left-hand point.

Fold one of the top points down, so it is flat against the other folds. Turn the cup over and fold the other top point down to make the cup shape.

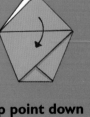

Open out your cup and fill it with water. Use patterned paper for some really wacky water holders!

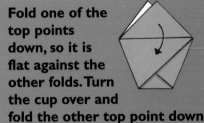

SCULPTING PAPER

Paper sculpture is lots of fun. Using just a few simple techniques, you can discover the secret of how to turn a sheet of plain paper into a 3-D picture!

P aper sculpture isn't like origami or papier-mâché, because you don't have to follow lots and lots of folding instructions, or wait ages for your finished piece of artwork to dry! Take a look at the techniques opposite and then, watch your paper sculptures take shape right before your eyes!

Cutting

To cut a sheet of paper cleanly, draw a fine pencil line where you wish to cut. Then, cut with a long, smooth motion using the whole length of the scissors' blades along the line. Don't cut to the ends of the blades though, or your paper will look hacked at!

Folding

To fold a piece of paper in half exactly, first match up the two edges. Then, smooth the palm of your hand towards the bent edge to make a gentle crease. Finally, run the edge of a ruler along the crease for a sharp fold.

Get sculpting
Why not try sculpting some funny features for paper people's faces

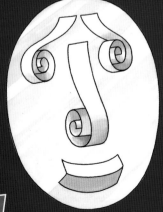

Mrs. Happy

Mr. Glum

Miss Surprised

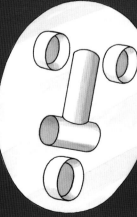

Curl Mrs. Happy's nose and eyes from paper strips and score her curving mouth.

Curl a sheet to make a a pouty mouth, then score a nose to give Mr. Glum a gloomy look.

Miss Surprised's face is just glued paper tubes.

Curling sheets

To curl a sheet of paper, place it on a table and lay one hand on the edge furthest from you. With the other hand, pull the sheet over the edge of the table and down towards the floor.

Gluing

Big blobs of glue will spoil your paper sculpture. Use a toothpick to put the glue exactly where you want it. By sticking the edges of a curled sheet of paper, you can make a perfect tube.

Curling strips

Curling a strip of paper is a little different. Instead of using the edge of a table, you use the edge of a closed pair of scissors. Drag the strip of paper between your thumb and the scissors for a springy curl!

Scoring straight lines

To make a neat crease in a piece of paper, you need to score it first. Use a ballpoint pen with the ink removed to rule a line along the edge of a ruler. Your paper will now crease perfectly along the scored line.

Scoring curved lines

Scoring the line for a curved crease is just as easy. Simply draw a light pencil line where you want the curved crease to be and then go over it with the empty ballpoint pen. Carefully fold the paper along the line.

Trace or copy these shapes and turn them into some fab face furniture!

Cut out a pair of ears.

Snip around the edge of a paper beard.

Sculpt some glasses from folded paper!

Frill some bushy eyebrows.

Groovy granny

Oops! I've gone and made a spectacle of myself again!

ha ha! How do bees keep their hair tidy? With honey-combs!

It's a stick-up! Make this flower-power granny with cut-out magazine pics. Then, add a pair of super specs!

What you need:

★ Sheet of thin blue card (14" x 14") ★ Pencil ★ Old gardening, furniture and food magazines ★ Scissors ★ Glue stick ★ Small sheet of thin card ★ Tracing paper ★ Ruler ★ Sheet of glossy red card (10" x 3½") ★ Cellophane ★ Small piece of pink paper

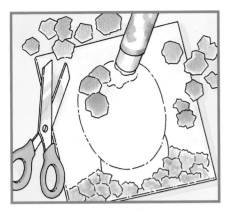

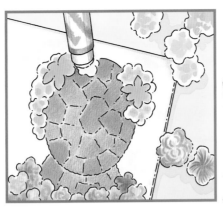

1 On the blue card, outline the granny's head and shoulders. Cut out purple flowers from magazines and stick them over the shoulders. Use brown pieces for the face and neck.

2 Cut out big, single flowers in shades of pink for the necklace. Use white and yellow scraps to form the hair – try daffodils, narcissi and lilies. You could even add a bee or two!

3 Cut out some red petal shapes to stick down in a curve for the mouth. Make sunflower eyes with yellow petals and a black circle. Find a bright red flower for the nose.

4 Cut out two matching brown ears. Glue these on to thin card for extra strength. Fold them in half. Glue down the bottom half of each ear and a pair of flower earrings.

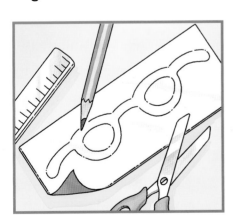

5 To make a pair of glasses, place tracing paper over your collage and sketch a pair to fit. Trace or copy the outline on to the back of the glossy, red card and cut them out.

6 Cut out two semicircles of Cellophane and glue them to the back of the specs for lenses. Add some petal shapes from pink paper. Tuck the specs behind the tops of the ears.

How spec-tacular!

You could make a range of different specs to fit the same collage face. Why not turn your gran into…

…glam gran?
Cut out brightly-colored ovals to decorate corners or shape specs like stars.

…sporty gran?
Join two tennis rackets with a tennis ball or fill lenses with funky soccer-balls.

…super-cool gran?
For a designer look, give your granny stylish sunglasses with dark-colored frames.

Fantastic faces

Create more clever collages of people based on their hobbies.

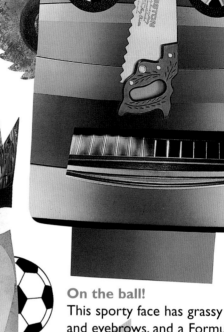

All tooled up!

This mean machine has a truly cutting-edge nose! Raid a catalog for cut-out collage scraps featuring hammers, wrenches and other handy features.

Music maestro

Find some sheet music as a background for this facial fanfare. Use guitar necks for spiky hair and a pair of CDs for eyes. Carefully cut out a violin to make a nose, and turn the top of a microphone upside-down to make an open, singing mouth.

On the ball!

This sporty face has grassy hair and eyebrows, and a Formula One headband. Cut out different balls for other fun features – soccer-ball eyes, a cricket-ball nose and a tennis-ball smile!

Yummy pets

Use food magazine cuttings to make some cool, animal collages.

Cakey cat

A scrummy, lemon tart is a great background for this feline face. Use strawberry tarts for eyes and a swirly meringue for the nose. Cut whiskery strips from a photo of a sticky flan.

Sausage dog

Two jumbo sausages make this hot dog's ears, but can you spot the third sausage? Trim most of the white off two fried eggs to make puppy-dog eyes that really boggle!

Funny bunny

Cut out circles of salad for this rabbit's face and cheeks. Use bundles of asparagus for its long ears and little pieces of celery for the goofy teeth.

28

Mask it!

Become a knight in shining armor with this foil helmet!

OOPS! Get an adult to help you cut out the helmet shape, the eye slit and the holes for the elastic.

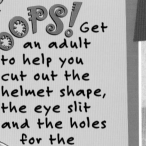

Ask an adult to enlarge this template on a photocopier for your feathers.

What you need:

★ Cardboard box (at least 8" × 4" × 4")
★ Ruler ★ Pencil ★ Scissors
★ Use of an enlargement photocopier
★ Tracing paper ★ Sheet of red tissue paper ★ White glue ★ 3 pipe cleaners
★ Rubber band ★ Sticky tape
★ Newspaper ★ Kitchen foil
★ Short length of elastic

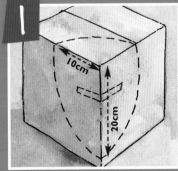

1 From the corner of the box, mark 4" along two of the top sides and 8" down the front. Join the marks with curved lines. Add a slit for the eyes. Cut out mask.

10cm
20cm

2 Trace three, enlarged feathers on to tissue paper. Glue pipe cleaners along dotted lines. Snip feathery edges. Tie with a rubber band and tape to the top of mask.

3 Screw newspaper into balls and stick them around the feathers with tape. Mold the foil over the mask and secure it firmly at the back with tape.

4 Poke the foil through the eye slit. Ask an adult to attach the elastic to either side of the mask. Roll up eight tiny balls of foil for rivets. Glue them around the mask.

Junk jeep

Make a mini, match box car so that your toys can travel in style!

What you need:
★ A large, empty match box
★ Scissors ★ Pencil ★ Glue stick ★ A large, round coin
★ Poster paints in white, red, yellow, green and black

ha ha!
What happened when the frog's car broke down?

It got toad away!

1 Remove the outer sleeve from the match box and cut it in half. To make it easier, cut up one side, turn the scissors and cut around the sleeve.

2 Make two cuts on either side of the sleeve top. Bend the flap forward for a windshield. Glue halfway along the sides of the draw. Slide the sleeve on top.

3 For wheels, draw around a large coin four times on the leftover half of the matchbox sleeve. Cut them out and glue them to your jeep.

4 Cover the whole jeep in white poster paint. When it's dry, outline head-lights and a grill in pencil. Now you can give your jeep a custom paint job!

Pretty pendant!

Make a silvery leaf necklace to wear on special occasions.

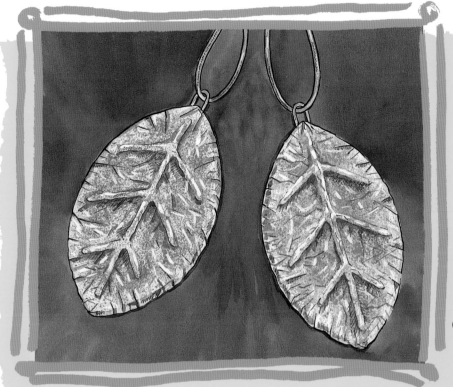

What you need:

* Small piece of thin card
* Pencil * Scissors * Paperclip
* White glue * String * Sheet of silver foil * Thin paintbrush
* Acrylic paints in pink and blue
* Saucers
* Small piece of sponge

ha ha! How does an elephant get down from a tree? Sits on a leaf and waits for autumn!

OOPS! Let each layer dry before painting another.

1 Make a simple leaf template and copy it twice on to thin card. Cut out. Put the paperclip between the two leaves with the end poking out. Glue together.

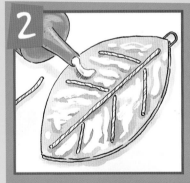

2 Cut several short pieces of string. Cover one side of the leaf with glue. Stick on the lengths of string to make the leaf's veins.

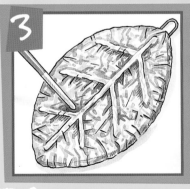

3 Screw up and open the foil. Wrap it around the leaf, shiny side up. Trim off any extra bits. Mold it tightly over the string with the end of the paintbrush.

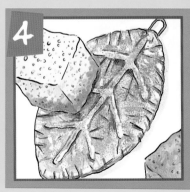

4 Dab paint on to the leaf with the sponge. Build up layers of color. Thread a long piece of string through the paperclip and tie a knot.

TESSELLATION ✓
COLLAGE ✓
COLORING ✓

Color class

Baby mad!

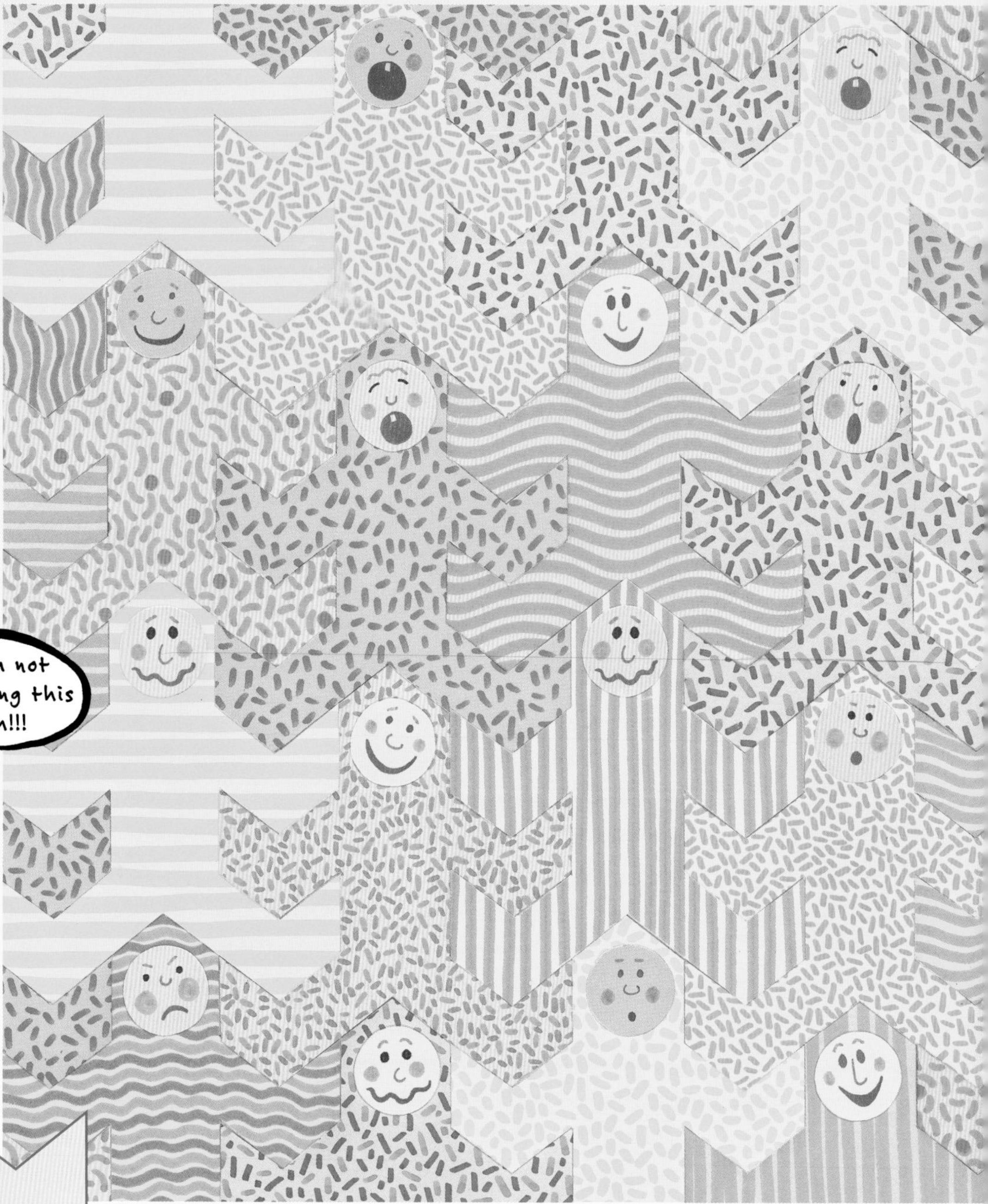

These boggling babes will send you ga-ga! The clever shapes tessellate, which means they all fit together exactly.

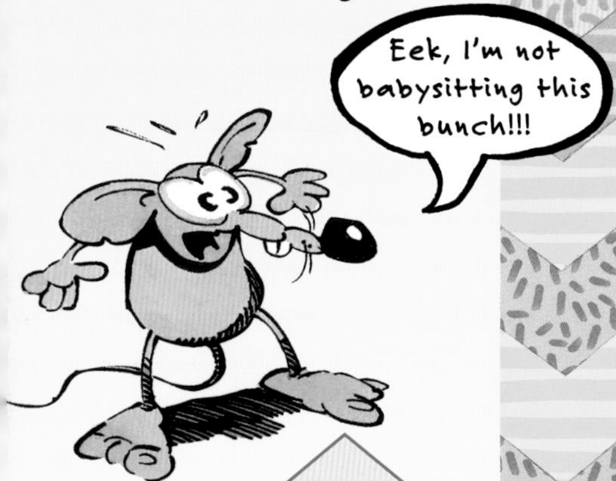

Eek, I'm not babysitting this bunch!!!

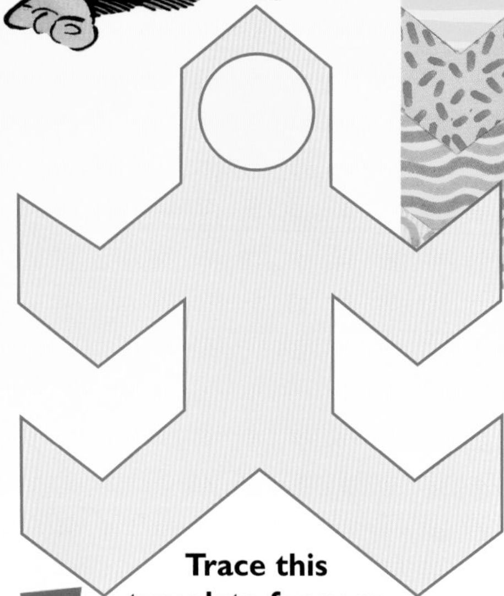

Trace this template for your picture.

What you need:

★ 8 sheets of letter size paper in pale yellow, blue, green and pink ★ Felt-tip pens ★ Tracing paper ★ Pencil ★ Small sheet of card ★ Scissors ★ Sheet of white paper ★ Glue stick

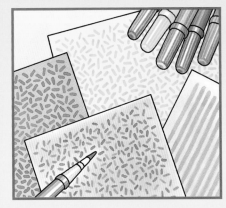

1 Using felt-tip pens, make a different pattern on each sheet of colored paper. Try out dashes in all directions and straight or wavy stripes.

2 Trace the baby template on to the sheet of card. Trace the circle for the face separately. Cut out both card templates very carefully.

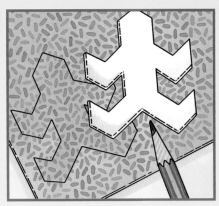

3 Draw around the body template on the patterned paper. On the striped paper, turn the template so the babies have stripes down and across.

4 Cut out the babies and glue them to the paper. Make sure their bodies interlock and no two babies with the same pattern touch.

5 Using the round template, cut out circles in different colored paper. Draw on funny faces with felt-tip pens and glue them to the bodies.

6 Snip off any arms and legs that go over the edge of the paper and use leftover scraps of patterned paper to fill in gaps between the babies.

Fishy flow!

Curvy creatures are so easy to fit together! Just join these jolly fish nose-to-tail and go with the flow!

Better tessellate than never!

33

Take two shapes...

You'll be amazed at how many different patterns you can create using these two simple templates – an octagon and a square.

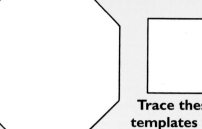

Trace these templates for your pictures.

Dancing crabs
Use blue squares for the sea, and orange and yellow octagons for the crabs and sand. Then draw in the pincers, legs and eyes with felt-tip pens so that the crabs face each other diagonally!

Spider web
Pattern the octagons in shades of pink and purple. Turn the purple ones into spiders by giving each one oggling eyes and eight legs using a felt-tip pen.

Check this!
For these terrific terrapins, use different green checks alongside wavy lines. Make each row face in opposite directions.

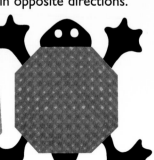

ha ha!
What do you call an ant with frog's legs?
An ant-phibian!

34

MOSAICS

All you need to create your own amazing mosaic effects is paper, glue and a bit of patience!

A mosaic is a pattern or picture made up of tiny pieces stuck closely together. Throughout history, craftsmen have used stone, glass, marble and even gold to build mosaics for their walls and floors. But you can make beautiful patterns with colored paper and card.

Use different types of paper or card to make a mosaic.

Old magazine pages are multicolored.

Gummed paper doesn't need gluing.

Ready-cut, gummed squares come in packets.

Careful cuts

Making your mosaic is simple if you cut up the squares before you begin. Mark out the squares lightly with a pencil and ruler ($\frac{1}{2}$" x $\frac{1}{2}$" is a good size). Next, cut along the lines to make strips and cut up the strips to make squares. Assembling your mosaic will be easier if you color code your squares, putting all the shades of one color together in a saucer.

Piece it together

It's best to start with a simple, geometric design for your first mosaic. Use a ruler to draw a border around the edge of a square sheet of card. Then, add a diamond in the middle.

Work on one section of your mosaic at a time. Put some glue in a saucer and use an old brush to cover the section with glue and stick down your squares, one by one. Make sure that they all fit together closely.

Trace or photocopy the patterns above and use them as guides for your own mosaic borders.

Jumbo party straws

Make these fun party straws that your friends will never forget!

Trace the... Place on fold of paper ...your straws.

What you need:

★ Thick white paper
★ Tracing paper
★ Pencil and scissors
★ Felt-tip pens in blue, orange and black
★ Drinking straws
★ Sticky tape

1 Fold a piece of white paper in half. Trace the elephant on to the paper, with the left-hand side of the tracing against the fold. Cut the shape out.

2 Open out the elephant and draw on some daisies like the one here in the corner. Color around the eyes, tusks and daisies with a blue felt-tip pen.

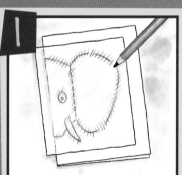

3 Color the centers of the daisies orange, and add black pupils in the elephant's eyes. Fold its ears forward along the dotted lines.

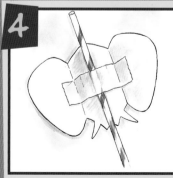

4 Tape a drinking straw to the back of the elephant's head. The end of the straw should stick out 2″ above the top. Try other patterns too.

Shadow puppets

Put on your own shadow puppet show!

To set up the screen, tape a large sheet of tracing paper under the top of a table. Get an adult to place a lamp behind the paper. Move your puppets around behind the screen to make them dance!

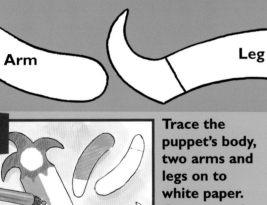

Arm

Leg

What you need:

★ Tracing paper ★ Pencil
★ White letter size paper
★ Scissors ★ Felt-tip pens in blue, pink, green, yellow, orange, and purple
★ Vegetable oil
★ Soft cloth
★ Hole punch
★ Paper fasteners
★ Sticky tape
★ 2 plant sticks

Trace or copy these templates and use them for your puppet.

1  Trace the puppet's body, two arms and legs on to white paper. Cut out, and color both sides of each piece with felt-tip pens.

2 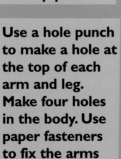 Using the soft cloth, rub a little vegetable oil over the front and back of each bit of the puppet to make them slightly see-through. Leave to dry.

3  Use a hole punch to make a hole at the top of each arm and leg. Make four holes in the body. Use paper fasteners to fix the arms and legs to the puppet's body.

4  Wrap some tape around the top of each plant stick, so it sticks out over the end. With another, shorter strip of tape, attach the sticks to the arms.

LETTERING TECHNIQUES

How can you make a word look like its meaning? Take a look at the lettering below and find out.

These two words (shown right) not only spell smaller and larger, they actually get smaller and larger, too! Shaping letters like this is easy. Draw two lines like a V shape turned on its side. Then, write your letters to fit between the lines. It's simple! For a really fabulous effect, shade your letters so that the small ones are the palest. This makes them look far away!

Round and round

Writing on straight lines can get boring! Try drawing a spiral and make your writing follow the curve. Why not write a spiralling letter to a friend?

 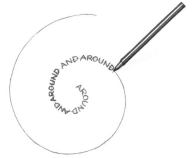

Cool curves
You can use saucers to draw guidelines for some curvy writing.

Use a large saucer, or a small plate to draw a curve at the corner of your page.

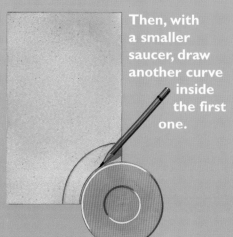

Then, with a smaller saucer, draw another curve inside the first one.

Write your words between the two lines for really curvy lettering.

MAKING MARGINS

As well as changing the shape of your letters, you can change the shape of a whole page of writing.

Cut four strips of card, each one slightly longer than your page. Tape them at the corners.

Lie the frame on your page and write inside it. When you take away the frame, you'll have an even border.

Try giving your card strips spiky or wavy edges to make really zany borders!

Tidal templates

Want to make a wacky, wavy word? Copy or trace this wave shape on to some card and use it as a guide to write along. Use a sea blue colored felt-tip pen. Try making some different crazy templates of your own.

Word pictures

Did you know that you can write a picture?

Draw a faint outline of a triangle with a pencil. Then, use a red felt-tip pen to write the word triangle inside it. Erase your pencil lines.

Try these other word pictures. Once you know how, it's easy!

Write on!

So, now you know how to draw a word, you can have some real fun! Think hard about what a word means before you draw it. Add speed lines to make the word 'speed' zip across your page! Put a bit of boing into the word 'bounce'. And make the word 'boom' really explode!

POP-UP CARDS

Learn how to make cool pop-up cards so you can send your friends an eye-catching surprise

To make your pop-ups work, always start with a sheet of thin card. You'll need the sheet to be twice as wide as the front of the finished card because you have to fold it!

Magic Marilyn

Marilyn's always up to mischief, popping up when you least expect it!

Trace or copy Marilyn and the pot on to card. Color them and cut them out. Cut a piece of card in half lengthways. Fold both pieces in half to make two cards. Decorate the front of one and lay the pot on it.

Mark the top and base of the pot on the card. Ask an adult to cut slits along the lines. Glue on the pot and slide Marilyn through the slits. Spread glue on the edges of the plain card and stick it inside the Marilyn card. Then, make Marilyn jump!

Springy Cedric

This springy, Cedric spiral is simple to make and gives your message real boing!

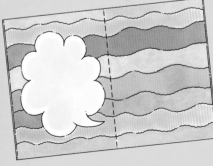

Trace or copy the curly Cedric on to thin card. Color him in and cut him out. Glue the first 5″ of his tail to the right-hand side of the open card. Write your message in his speech bubble. Open the card and Cedric springs out!

Fold a sheet of card in half. Open it and draw a speech bubble on the left-hand side. Cover the inside and outside of the card with a felt-tip pen pattern and add a greeting on the front.

Nice to sssee you!

FUNNY FOLD OUT

Send a friend a super Cedric slinking in the grass!

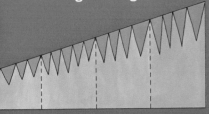

Cut the top left corner from a sheet of green card (4″ x 11½″), as above. Lightly mark out four equal sections. Draw and cut out grass along the top.

Trace or copy Cedric on to a piece of thin card. Color him in and cut him out.

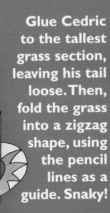

Glue Cedric to the tallest grass section, leaving his tail loose. Then, fold the grass into a zigzag shape, using the pencil lines as a guide. Snaky!

Fat rat regards

Fancy sending a special fat rat greeting? This Marilyn pop-up card's perfect!

1

Fold paper in half widthways. Fold a corner, as shown, leaving a 1″ strip at the edge, then open out the sheet.

2

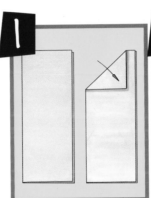

Trace or copy a fat Marilyn in the top half, with her head in the V. Cut from the edges to the fold at her shoulders.

3

Cut around her head. Fold the card back just below her feet. Close it, pulling her head forward. Open it and she pops up!

Postcard Pop-up

Use a postcard to make a brilliant, birthday surprise!

Draw a bang on card and fold it in half. Cut a strip of pink card (1½″ x 5″). Fold it in the middle and 1″ from each end.

Stick the ends of the strip either side of the fold on the card, as shown, to make a pop-up square. Leave it to dry.

Draw and color your birthday wishes on a postcard. Glue it to the front face of the pop-up square. Now, when the card is opened, your message will burst out!

Tropical card

Spread some sunshine! Make a great greeting card with a silhouette palm tree and a brilliant sunset.

Copy the tree here to go on your card.

What you need:

★ 2 sheets of card, one blue, one black ★ Pencil ★ Ruler ★ Scissors ★ White crayon ★ Glue stick ★ Green, blue and gold glitter ★ Paintbrush ★ Saucers ★ Poster paints in yellow, orange and pink

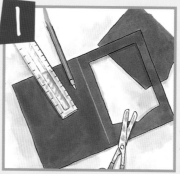

1 Use a ruler to draw a line down the middle of the card. On the right-hand side, cut out a window frame with a curved bottom edge.

2 Copy the palm tree shape on to black card. Use a white colored pencil so the outline shows up. Cut it out and glue on stripes of green and blue glitter.

3 Stick the palm tree across the window frame, on the left-hand side. Draw wavy lines with a glue stick below the tree, and stick on gold glitter for the beach.

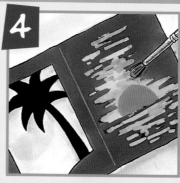

4 When the glue has dried, turn over the card and paint a sunset on the inside. Wait for the paint to dry, then fold the card so the tree is at the front.

Welcome home

Make a fun house and fill it with your family, friends and pets.

What you need:

★ Sheet each of red, orange and white card ★ Glue stick ★ String ★ Sticky tape ★ Tracing paper (optional) ★ Pencil ★ Scissors ★ Colored pencils ★ Photographs

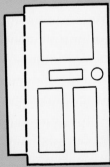

Trace or copy these templates and use them for your house.

 Ask an adult before you cut up any photographs!

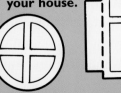

1 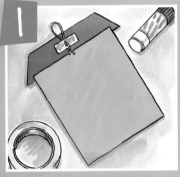 Cut a rectangle 5" x 5¾" from orange card and a red roof shape to fit on top. Glue the roof down. Tape a loop of string to the back to hang it up by.

2  Trace or copy the door and the window templates on to white card. Cut them out and color them in with colored pencils on both sides.

3 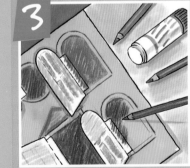 Lay the door and windows on your house and draw around them. Bend the flaps and glue in place. Color in the window and door outlines and add a porch.

4  Cut people and pets from photos and glue them in the windows. Cut a letterbox, cat flap and attic window from card and glue in place. Color a step and bricks.

Circuit chase

Paint this ace, racetrack game. Then, roll the dice and follow the instructions, to race your bikes from start to finish!

PITS

13

14

15 Tire change—go to pits for 2 turns

16

17

18

19 Oil—skid on 4 spaces

20

12

11

10

9

8 CRASH! miss a turn

7

6

5 Rev up—move on a space

4

3 Go back to start

2

1

FINISH

START

STANDS

SKID CORNER

What you need:
★ sheet of cardboard ★ Pencil ★ Poster paints in green, yellow, orange, gray, black, white and red ★ Felt-tip pens in black, red, blue, yellow and green ★ Tracing paper (optional) ★ Small piece of white card ★ Air-dry Clay

How to play: Take turns to roll the dice and move your bike, following any instructions which you land on. The winner is the person who reaches the checkered-flag finish space first. If the number you roll takes you past the finish, you have to go around again!

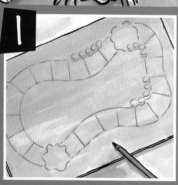

1 Copy the track outline on to the cardboard. Draw the oil spill, stands, crash, pits and tires. Divide the rest of the track into 22 roughly equal spaces.

2 Paint the background green. Add flags and paint the spaces orange, yellow and white, as shown above. Outline the track with a black felt-tip pen.

3 Use a red felt-tip pen to draw arrows on the start space. Use a black pen to number the spaces, write on the instructions and draw the checkered finish.

4 Trace or copy two motorbikes from the border on to white card. Color them in and cut them out. Press them into the clay to make them stand up.

Hoppity hop!

Make this wiggly frog dance in your hands!

What you need:
★ Pencil ★ Tracing paper (optional) ★ Sheet of thick, white paper ★ Felt-tip pens ★ Scissors ★ White glue ★ Clothes pin ★ Pipe cleaner ★ Sticky tape

Trace or copy this frog for your model.

1 Copy or trace the frog's body and one leg on to the paper. Reverse the template to trace or copy the other leg. Color the frog in. Cut it out.

2 Using glue, stick one of the frog's legs on to one half of the clothes peg. Stick the other leg on to the other half.

3 Thread a pipe cleaner through the holes in the top of the peg. Then bend both ends of the pipe cleaner in towards the middle of the clothes pin, as shown.

4 Place strips of tape under the pipe cleaner, sticky side up. Attach the frog's body to the tape. Open and close to see the frog's legs move!

Crazy card cactus

What could be handier for hanging things than a cactus with big branches?

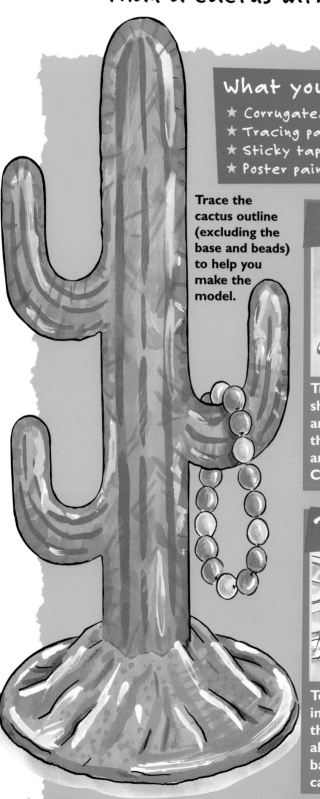

Trace the cactus outline (excluding the base and beads) to help you make the model.

What you need:

★ Corrugated card (the side of an old cardboard box will do)
★ Tracing paper (optional) ★ Pencil ★ Saucer ★ Scissors
★ Sticky tape ★ Newspaper ★ Flour and water paste in a bowl
★ Poster paints in green and orange ★ Medium paintbrush

1

Trace or copy this cactus shape on to the card. Add an extra 1" for a flap at the bottom. Next, draw around a small saucer. Cut out both shapes.

2

Fold over the flap at the bottom of the cactus and tape it to the card circle. Use enough tape to make the cactus stand up and not fall over.

3

Tear some newspaper into small strips. Scrunch them up and tape them all over the cactus and base. Continue until your cactus is well padded out.

4

Dip newspaper strips in the flour and water paste, and cover the cactus to give a smooth finish. Leave to dry, then paint green and orange.

FABRIC PAINTING

I wish someone would invent some sssnake paint!

Brighten up fabric by brushing on paint, squeezing it out of a tube, or even scribbling with special pastels. It's all terrific fun!

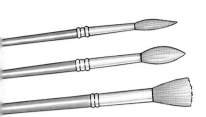
Try out different sized paintbrushes for various effects.

Fabric paint pastels are perfect for scribbling!

You can buy little jars of fabric paint from most craft shops.

Squeezy bottles are great for painting lines.

Fabric paints come in every color that you can think of. They make a great change from painting on paper and they liven up all sorts of material things. Try painting on T-shirts or turning tired old sneakers into truly cool footwear!

Getting started

You need to keep your fabric stretched flat while you paint. Tape two pieces of thick card together for a sturdy board, then pin your fabric on to it. Cover the sewing pins with masking tape to stop your hands catching on them and you're ready to paint! Practice some funky colored patterns on paper before you start on the real thing.

Cover your work surface with lots of newspaper!

STOP!

Fruity fun   Each kind of fabric paint creates its own cool effect.

Use a squeezy bottle of fabric paint to draw an apple outline minus a bite! Squeeze lines for the leaf and highlights. Crunchy!

Pots of fabric paint are best for painting blocks of color. This rosy, red apple is just made from three shapes. Tasty!

OOPS! Ask an adult to iron the fabric when it is dry to fix the paint.

Cut out a card stencil and tape it over your fabric. Scribble shade with fabric pastels. Juicy!

Color class

Doodle bug

Paint yourself a cool insect T-shirt. It's simply eye-buggling!

What you need:

★ White T-shirt ★ Sheet of card (about ½" wider than the T-shirt)
★ Masking tape ★ Sheet of paper
★ 2B pencil ★ Scissors
★ 2 small sponges ★ Ordinary fabric paints in green, red and blue
★ Medium and thin paintbrushes
★ Cork ★ Dimensional fabric paint in pearlized blue

Painting your T-shirt

● Wash and dry a new T-shirt, before painting it.

● Iron the T-shirt, then fold it so that the sleeves match and iron over the crease. Center your design on the crease.

● Put card inside the T-shirt to stop the paint seeping through and to make the T-shirt stretch flat. Remove it when the paint is dry.

● Tape the T-shirt firmly to your work surface.

● Follow your paint instructions exactly. You may need to paint the flat colors then fix them by ironing before you add the dimensional details.

Copy these templates the size you want for the bug on your T-shirt.

1 Fold the sheet of paper in half lengthways. Copy the head and body shapes the size you want for your T-shirt. Make sure they are on the folded edge! Cut them out to make a stencil.

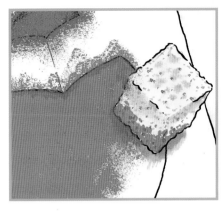

2 Unfold the stencil and tape it on to the middle of the T-shirt. Sponge on green fabric paint for the head and red paint for the body. Use a different sponge for each color.

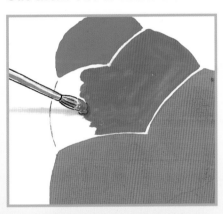

3 With a soft pencil, draw two curved lines to join the bug's head to its body. Carefully fill in this segment with blue fabric paint using a medium paintbrush.

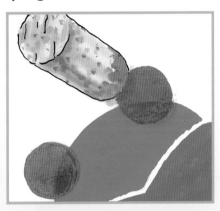

4 When the green fabric paint has dried, dip the flat end of the cork in red fabric paint. Use this to print two circular eyes on top of your insect's head.

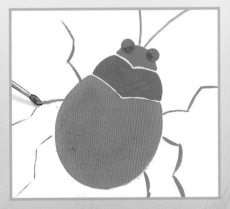

5 Sketch a pair of feelers in soft pencil coming from the bug's head. Using a thin brush, paint over the lines with blue fabric paint. Now draw six jointed legs. Paint these green.

6 Draw swirls on the bug's shell in soft pencil. Then squeeze blue pearlized dimensional paint over the lines. Use this paint to highlight the bug's eyes, too.

Insect inspiration

Once you get the bug, you'll want to decorate all your T-shirts! Try these ideas for size.

Sponge bug
This creepy-crawly couldn't be simpler! Use an oval sponge to print the body, then squeeze on the details with dimensional paint.

Hop to it!
An old, string bag makes an unusual stencil when you come to add the finishing touches to this grasshopper. Make sure the paint on your sponge is almost dry, or it will seep through the string.

ha ha!
What has a hundred legs and crawls on envelopes?

A stampede!

Shiny shield bug
Cut out a bug stencil, leaving only a thin space between the head and body. Use glitzy metallic paints.

Centipede swirl
Print this slinky centipede's segments with sponge printing blocks. Add on eyes, antennae and legs with a paintbrush.

Quick march!
Use a piece of modelling clay to print a snaking line of mini ladybug bodies. Add the black details with a paintbrush.

FUN FACTS

There are at least a million insects alive in the world for every human being!

The heaviest beetle in the world is the African Goliath beetle. This flying insect grows to about 4½" and can weigh up to 3½ ounces - as heavy as two golf balls.

The cave cricket from central Nigeria has mighty long antennae! Its feelers stretch six times the length of its 1" body to help it find its way around in dark caves.

Don't bug me!

Sock it to 'em!

"Snip and stick" an old sock to make a wonderful, woolly hand puppet!

What you need:

★ An old, plain-colored sock
★ Scissors ★ Double-sided sticky tape ★ Lengths of blue and red yarn (about 3½" long) ★ Tracing paper (optional) ★ Pencil ★ Black felt ★ Strip of card (4" x 6")
★ Acrylic paints in white and black ★ Medium paintbrush
★ 2 saucers

Use this template for ears on your hand puppet.

1  Cut along the sock from the heel to the bottom of the elastic. Stick a strip of double-sided sticky tape along the inside and peel off the backing.

2 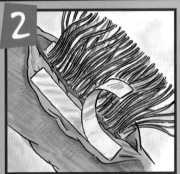 Lay lengths of colored yarn along the tape. Stick another piece of tape along the other side of the cut. Peel off backing to stick the two sides together.

3  Trace the ear shape and cut it out. Use it as a guide to cut two black felt ears. With double-sided sticky tape, stick the edges by the points together.

4  Push a strip of card into the sock. Stick the ears in position with double-sided sticky tape. Paint on white eyes, then black stripes, a nose and pupils.

Treasure train

Make a train for your money and your secrets!

What you need:
* ★ Ruler ★ Use of an enlargement photocopier
* ★ Rectangular cardboard box with lid (like a shoe box)
* ★ Scissors ★ Pencil ★ Tracing paper ★ Sheet of thin, white card ★ Felt-tip pens in red, green and black ★ White glue

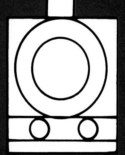

Enlarge these templates on a photocopier, then trace them and use them for your money box.

1

Measure your box, and get an adult to help you enlarge the templates on a photocopier to fit it. Cut a slit in the lid to use as a slot for your money.

2

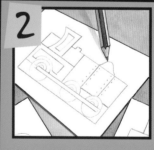

Trace the side of the train on to the card. Turn the tracing paper over to draw the other side. Trace the front and back views of the train.

3

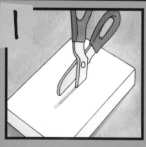

Color in the train with felt-tip pens. Go over the outline and details with the black felt-tip pen. Now carefully cut out all the pieces of the train.

4

Glue the lid to the box. Then glue the train pieces to the sides of the box. The edges should go over the rim of the lid and all line up. Leave to dry.

Mouse-work

Keep your string tidy in this easy-to-make, mouse tin! Squeaky clean!

What you need:

★ Clean, tube-shaped, cardboard container with a lid ★ Medium paintbrush ★ Blue acrylic paint ★ Sheet of paper in orange, yellow and red ★ Pencil ★ Compass ★ Ruler ★ Scissors ★ White glue ★ Small, round white stickers ★ Felt-tip pens in black and red ★ Ball of string ★ Clay

1 Paint the tube blue. Draw two large, round orange bodies, a smaller, yellow head and two red ears, with a compass on the colored paper. Cut them out.

2 Glue the two body circles to opposite sides of the tube. On one side, glue ears peeping up over the top of the tube. Glue the head in the middle.

3 Use three small, round stickers for a nose and eyes. Color the pupils and a red nose with felt-tip pens. Glue three pieces of string on either side of the nose.

4 To make a hole for the tail, push a pencil through the tube in to a clay ball. Put your string in the tube. Pull the free end out of the hole. Replace the lid.

Color class

Curly whirly!

Discover the thrills of quills with this magical, mermaid pic.

Quilling ...technique

Rule lines, about ¼″ apart, across sheets of colored paper. Cut them into strips. To make a curly quill, wrap a strip tightly around the end of a paintbrush. Gently unravel it. For an S shape, curl the end of a curly quill in the opposite direction.

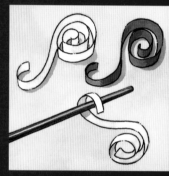

What you need:
★ Sheets of colored paper in cream, gray, yellow, red, dark pink, orange, blue, green, dark blue and white ★ Sheet of turquoise paper, at least 9½″ x 8″ ★ Pencil ★ Scissors ★ Black felt-tip pen ★ White glue ★ Ruler ★ Paintbrush

1 Draw a mermaid's body on cream paper, with a face, waistline and belly button. Draw a rock on gray paper and a circle on yellow paper.

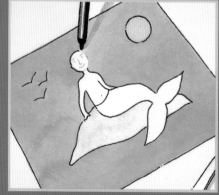

2 Cut them out and stick them on to turquoise paper, using the finished picture as a guide. Go over the pencil lines with a black felt-tip pen.

3 Use S-shaped yellow and red quills for the sun's rays and curly yellow quills for hair. Spread glue on the area, then gently press down the quills.

4 Spread glue all over the mermaid's tail. Carefully stick down tightly-curled quills in red, dark pink and orange paper to make the fishy scales.

5 Glue blue and green quills on the rock for seaweed. Add three seagulls, made from short white strips folded in half and curled slightly at the tips.

6 Finally, stick on the waves. Use dark blue, S-shaped quills for the water and white for the surf. Glue them all facing the same way. Leave to dry.

55

All at sea

Quilling is the perfect technique for making all sorts of swirly sea creatures!

Legs a go-go!

Use yellow quills to make this awesome octopus. First, cut out a green octopus shape. Then, draw an outline in felt-tip pen and stick on white, boggly eyes!

Star stunner

Use red quills against an orange paper background for this super starfish!

High flyer

Blue quills on a yellow background make this flying fish really leap out at you!

Jolly jelly

Use long and loose purple curls for spectacular jellyfish tentacles. Curl tighter quills for the body.

Mermaid's purse

Use a blue felt-tip pen to draw long swirls from the corners of this pink and blue mermaid's purse.

FUN FACTS

Flying fish can remain airborne for up to 40 seconds! They propel themselves out of the water at speeds of 20mph. Getting out of the sea is a good way to escape a hungry predator!

Mermaid's purse is the name given to the case that fish, such as skate, keep their eggs safe in before they hatch.

If a starfish loses an arm, it simply grows a new one! Star-tling!

Most starfish have five arms, but some can have up to 50!

Octopuses can open screw-top jars and stoppered bottles to get at food inside.

One record-breaking Pacific giant octopus had a tentacle span of 31 feet!

Groovy headwear!

Get in the swing of things with this star-spangled headband.

What you need:
- ★ Pencil ★ Tracing paper (optional) ★ 2 sheets of white 11" x 17" paper ★ Scissors
- ★ Sheet of red 8½" x 11" paper
- ★ Ruler ★ White glue ★ Red and blue felt-tip pens
- ★ Sticky tape
- ★ Paper clip

Trace or copy these stars for your templates.

1  Trace or copy five big stars from the template on to one sheet of white paper. Carefully cut them out for the dangling decorations.

2  Cut five strips of different lengths from red paper. Make them at least 8" long and ¾" wide. Glue a star to the end of each one.

3  Cut out a 2½" wide headband from white paper, long enough to go around your head with ends overlapping. Add stars and stripes then color in.

4 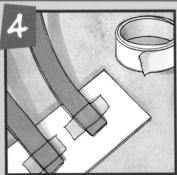 Tape the ends of the red strips to the inside of the headband. Use a paper clip to fasten the ends of the headband together so it fits your head.

Firework display

Whoosh! These fireworks light up the sky! Make your own bonfire night by scratching black paint off a crayon pattern.

What you need:

★ Sheet of white paper
★ Wax crayons in bright colors
★ Poster paint in black
★ Saucer
★ A few drops of dish washing liquid
★ Paintbrush
★ Popsicle stick
★ Toothpick

Follow these tips for a brilliant scratch picture…

● Make sure you don't leave gaps in your wax crayon pattern, as paint won't scratch off any areas of plain, unwaxed paper.

● Leave the black paint to dry completely before you start scratching it off – if it's wet, your picture will smudge.

● Experiment – scratch away paint with different objects, like a fork or a coin.

1 **On a sheet of white paper, use bright wax crayons to make a pattern of large blocks of color.**

You may need several coats of black paint!

2 **Next, in a saucer, mix a little black paint with a couple of drops of dish washing liquid. Then paint over your pattern. Leave it to dry.**

3 **Using a popsicle stick, scratch off the black paint so the colors underneath show through. Scratch out clusters of lines to make fireworks.**

4 **Use a toothpick to scratch out thinner lines and sparks of light. Scratch off some swirls for pinwheels and fountains for Roman candles.**

5 **To finish off your picture, scratch out some long, straight lines for rockets shooting across the sky, and add more tiny sparks of light.**

Scratch pictures

You can make mini scratch pictures of anything and everything! Here are a few ideas…

Color class

Cool cat!

Andy Warhol is famous for his Pop Art repeat prints of soup tins. But he also did lots of purr-fect cat prints. Make your own brilliant Pop Art cat.

ha ha!
What do cats eat for breakfast?

Mice Krispies!

What you need:

★ Tracing paper ★ HB pencil ★ 3 sheets of white card (10" × 10") ★ White glue ★ Scissors ★ Thick colored paper in red, dark blue, bright blue, yellow, orange and purple ★ Crayons in different colors

1 Trace the cat on to two sheets of white card. Follow the dark blue outlines around the paper shapes. Ignore the red lines.

2 Carefully number each section of the cat, even the tiniest ones, on each sheet. Glue one tracing on to a third piece of card for strength.

3 From this thicker card, cut out each section of the cat (you could use nail scissors for the small, fiddly pieces). These are your collage templates.

4 Draw around the templates on the colored papers (you decide the colors) and cut out. Write down the right number on the back of each piece.

5 Match the numbers on your colored card shapes to the numbers on the cat on the uncut white card. Glue each section in place.

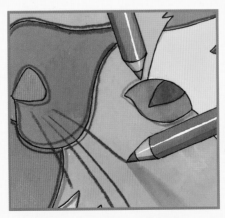

6 To finish off, go over the edges of each section of your Pop Art collage in crayons. Don't forget to draw in some whiskers!

Quickdraw
...a cat

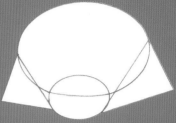

Sketch two ovals. Add a triangle on each side.

Draw ears and eye outlines. Fill in the nose and mouth in the smaller oval. Erase any unwanted lines.

Add the pupils. Give the face a jagged, furry outline. Sketch in eyebrows and cheekbones.

Shade the nose, then add a nose, furry neck and whiskers.

Feline groovy!

Try copying and cutting colored paper shapes from this gallery of collage cats. Use fewer sections to make it easier.

Creamy Siamese

Cream and brown make fur purr-fection – but don't forget you'll need a brilliant blue for this cat's eyes.

Smoky Persian

Try using shades of grey and orange for this elegant pussycat – and remember to make him really fluffy!

Ginger tom

Every cat's different, but shades of orange, red and yellow have been used for this tomcat.

FUN FACTS

🐾 The smallest pet cat is a Himalayan Persian called Tinker Toy. He's just 3" tall and 7½" long (less than the width of this page!)

🐾 In the dark, cats can see miles better than humans. This is because their pupils widen to let in every last bit of available light.

🐾 Odd-eyed White Persians have one blue eye and one orange eye. They're often deaf in the ear on the side of their blue eye! Now that is weird!

🐾 The Ragdoll is well-named. This long-haired cat goes totally floppy when it's picked up and resting in your arms!

🐾 Cats have five claws on each forepaw (and four on each back paw). The fifth, or dew claw, is actually a little way up the leg.

All about... FRAMING ARTWORK

All great artists know it's important to frame paintings properly. Visit any gallery and you'll be amazed by the effort put into the way each picture is displayed. Whether it's in a fancy gold frame or a simple surround, the way a picture is presented can really transform it. So why not give it a try and start your own exhibition?!

It's time to show off! Make the most of your masterpieces by following these framing tips.

Marvellous mounts

The easiest way to display your picture is with a mount. This is a simply a piece of card, on to which you stick your picture.

Measure your picture and then cut a piece of card slightly larger. Mark on the card where you would like the picture to go. It's usual to leave a bigger space at the bottom of your card than at the top. Stick down your picture within your marks.

When you've stuck your picture down, you could use a felt-tip pen to draw a decorative line around it.

Use three different colored pieces of card and cut each one a little smaller than the first. Stick them one on top of the other, and your picture will leap off the wall!

Themed scenes!

Surround your painting with another picture. Add sun, sea and clouds to your holiday pics, or pressed flowers to a painting of lilies.

Stick to it!

Go sticking crazy with bits and bobs! Buttons and gummed shapes are perfect for decorating a plain frame.

Acorn frame

Make clay stamps to print a great acorn frame for your pictures!

ha ha!

What's the best way to meet a squirrel?

Run up a tree and act nutty!

1 Make a clay leaf-shaped stamp. Press in the sides with your finger. Make two acorn shapes. Use a pencil to make indents on the shell part.

2 Cut a rectangle larger than your picture from thick, colored paper. Cut the center out of the rectangle to make a frame.

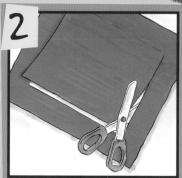

3 Dip the leaf stamp in pink poster paint and print a pattern of leaves on the frame. Print yellow and orange acorns in between.

4 Squeeze glue around the edge of your picture. Place the frame on top of the picture and press the edges firmly together.